I0171236

CHRISTIAN DATING

20 KEYS

TO HEALTHY RELATIONSHIPS

Karen Maloy, Ed.S.

Mutual Blessings Books
Huntsville, AL
MBSuccess@karenmaloy.org
www.karenmaloy.org

To order additional copies of this resource: write MB Success Strategies at MBSuccess@karenmaloy.org; call orders at (315) 657-3648 or order online at www.karenmaloy.org.

Printed in the United States of America

Unless otherwise indicated, all Scripture quotations are taken from the New International Version of the Bible.
Christian Dating: Twenty Keys to Healthier Relationships
Mutual Blessings Books
Publisher/Editor: MB Success Strategies
Published by Mutual Blessings - Huntsville, AL 35802
1-315-657-3648 - Website: **www.karenmaloy.org**

ISBN:
ISBN-13: **978-0-9856608-1-9**

DEDICATION

This book is dedicated to my children LaToya, Jemel, Myisha & Nyangel, and my grandchildren Meishawn, Myshon, Marliah, Messiah, and Breasia. May this book help you to avoid the mistakes I made in the process of growing up. I love you.

TABLE OF CONTENTS

SECTION 3:   RELATIONSHIP BUILDING

SECTION 4   BEFORE YOU SAY "I DO"

APPENDIX

Introduction

If you are like most Christians, you are confused about what to do about dating. You are tired of spending your time on relationships that start off okay but, over a period time they lose their luster and you end up with grief, heartache, and ill feelings that you carry onto your next relationship.

Maybe you are frustrated because you are tired of waiting, or you don't know how to find that right one for you. Perhaps you have been in a few serious relationships, only to find out that you wanted something more than they did. Or maybe you are single again after being in a committed relationship and are afraid of making the same mistakes. Whatever your reasons are makes no difference, and the stark reality is that you are entering (or re-entering) the dating stage of development.

Information has been limited when it comes to discovering how to date as a Christian, and while churches spend a lot of time teaching women how to live their lives according to Proverbs 31, nothing is available on the kind of man who is equipped to handle this kind of woman.

Believing that the church is the place to teach us how to live life on this earth, a resource is being offered to the Christian community to provide guidance in this area. The truths you find in this book will have a clear moral foundation based upon biblical scriptures, and if you choose to abide by the foundations which will be offered in this book, you will be able to protect yourself from the heartache and pain which is often associated with contemporary dating.

My vision is that this book will provide you with some basic guidelines which would help you to avoid the problems associated with modern dating strategies. This will increase your odds of a having a successful dating experience, provide the foundation needed for you to present yourself as a suitable mate, as well as equip you to build a healthy, loving, and lasting relationship with another individual. This book is necessary so that you can prepare for one of the most important relationships in your life – marriage.

Blessings – Minister Karen

Section 1
A Firm Foundation

ജ

God is not trying to ruin your life - He is trying to show you how to enjoy it!

Karen Maloy

ജ

1

Recognize the importance that God places on your happiness

Your happiness is not based on what you are but in who you know.

Whether we realize it or not, God is committed to our happiness. Created for God's glory, it is important for you to understand that you will not find happiness in anything that does not bring him glory.

You were created with the divine purpose of fellowshipping with God who is the source of your contentment.

All of creation (including you) was created to worship God but, you were specifically created for fellowship with God. Being restored to God's original intention for man through the blood of Jesus, you are now able to go face to face with God.

Without happiness, your life will be a painful existence.

God has a plan for your happiness. Just like living according to His word will bring happiness, unhappiness occurs when we choose the opposite. Unhappiness occurs as a result of us violating God's principles.

ဆလ

The type of relationships you nurture will determine where your life is heading.

Karen Maloy

ဆလ

2

Understand that your relationships have a divine purpose

Relationships are part of God's plan to bring fulfillment into your life.

The desire for human relationships is a basic human desire. We are not to try to place others in the place where God belongs in our lives, and we are also not to try to put God in the place where other people belong. Wisdom comes in knowing that God fulfills your spiritual needs, people fulfill your emotional, and when you get married, your physical needs.

God wants you to enjoy your relationships

If God did not want you to enjoy your relationships, he would not have given us so many examples in the Bible. There are different kinds of relationships, and they have their unique purposes. Wisdom is in knowing what kind of relationship it is, and to learn how to respond accordingly.

God sends people into your life to empower you.

In Hebrews 10:25, we learn that we are not to forsake
coming together in order to encourage one another. While
we have conveniently interpreted that as coming to church,
it is more of a principle to encourage saints to stay
connected with one another.

ഹോരു

The enemy is counting on you to be true to your [human] nature.

Karen Maloy

ഹോരു

3

Discern that Satan is the enemy of your life

As God's creation, you are also the focus of God's enemy.

As the result of the fall, all men were born into sin separated from God. The ploy of the enemy is to keep you blind to the truth. If Satan can keep you from reconciling with God, he can keep you from being happy.

By keeping you discontent, the enemy can control your life.

Many Christians are a slave to their emotions, which is makes it very easy for them to be influenced by the enemy. Much like Adam and Eve who chose to eat the forbidden fruit, if you cannot control yourself, you are ultimately giving control over to the enemy.

Satan sends people into your life to negatively influence you.

Satan is the great counterfeiter, using God principles to defeat you. God created us to desire fellowship with others, and he warns us about ungodly relationships clearly stating that they corrupt us. Use King Solomon as an example and be mindful of those you choose to fellowship with.

ജେ൝

If you want to defeat God's enemy, you must use God's tools.

Karen Maloy

ജെ൝

4

Know how to use your spiritual authority

Surround yourself with godly influences.

Know that there is power in the name of Jesus. In addition, we are promised that when we gather in his name, he is there with us. Therefore, if you surround yourself with godly influences, you are positioning yourself to have the power your need to halt the enemy's attack against you.

Anticipate and resist any negative influences in your life.

Be not unwise to Satan's devices. Once you know how he operates, you are now in a position to recognize any signs of a potentially negative influence in your life. Remember, it is Satan's goal to destroy you and your relationships. You have the responsibility to become a watchman on the tower of your own life.

Evaluate your relationships often to ensure that they are bringing glory to God.

Knowing that Christians are always under spiritual attack, we are always at risk of falling. Be mindful of people who are operating in habitual sin, for they are at risk of a hardened heart.

ഇൻജ

*If you do not
know how to
judge all
things rightly,
you will be
deceived.*

Karen Maloy

ഇൻജ

5

Pray for discernment daily

Recognize that Satan will bring people into your life to destroy it from the inside.

The Bible tells us to "guard our heart with all diligence" for a reason. If you reveal your heart, your soul and your weaknesses and they betray you, you cannot blame anyone else but yourself.

Discernment is God's way of revealing those people who are spoiled on the inside.

Not everything that looks good is good. Matthew 7:15 tells us "Beware of the false prophets, who come to you in sheep's clothing, but inwardly are ravenous wolves". This principle could also be applied in all of your relationships. Be mindful of people who appear to be someone that they are not.

Apply the blood of Jesus daily to protect you and your loved ones from the fiery darts of the enemy.

Make a habit of using the spiritual tools of warfare on a regular basis to protect your life and relationships from the attacks of your spiritual enemy.

Section 2
Positioning For Success

ೞೞ

*You can only
say that you
have learned
from your
mistakes if you
stop repeating
them, anything
else, you are
deceiving
yourself.*

Karen Maloy

ೞೞ

6

Make an Honest Assessment of Yourself

What you do not know about yourself will continue to drive you subconsciously.

Many people hold hidden hurts and pain from their childhood, which continue to plague them in their adult years. The purpose of this stage of development is to identify your strengths and weaknesses. If you do not know why you do the things that you do, you will not know what situations you need to avoid. If you do not take the time to evaluate yourself, your foundation will be based on faulty reasoning.

Becoming an honest person begins with being you honest with yourself.

The worst kind of deception is when you are deceiving yourself. Do not ask of others what we are not willing to give, and do not expect from others what cannot be expected of you. Portraying yourself to be someone that you are not now, will only lead to destruction later.

Faulty reasoning is the foundation for poor relationships.

Honesty is at the heart of every good relationship. This includes believing that you are someone that you are not. Believing that you are someone that you are not, are cracks in the foundation. Much like a building built upon a weak foundation, the damage will appear in the upper levels.

ଽଠେ

If you don't know what you want from your relationships, you don't what you will end up with.

Karen Maloy

ଽଠେ

7

Carefully plan what you want from your relationship

If you do not know what you want, others will tell you.

Before you enter your relationship you should already know what you want from it. Without that, you have no way of determining if you have the mate that you need to get to where you are going.

The only way to ensure that you get what you want is to plan for it.

Learn to develop offensive strategies. If you do not plan for it, you cannot blame anyone else if you do not get what you want.

Thinking about what you want starts you on a path of discovery.

Until you take the time to think about what you really want, you will never explore what it takes to get it.

ഔരു

A plan not written down is nothing more than wishful thinking.

Karen Maloy

ഔരു

8

Establish a list of what you will and will not tolerate

The only way to avoid relationship traps is to recognize them.

The reason that a trap is successful is because people step into them unaware. The only way to avoid a trap is to know how to recognize them. Learn how to recognize the behaviors on your *I will not tolerate* list.

Establishing a plan puts you in the driver's seat of your life.

It is the driver of the car who controls how to get to the destination. If you have not yet determined where you do not want to be, there is no way to measure if you are on the right road.

Identify potential warning signs.

The warning sign is only effective if the viewers know what it means when it is displayed. Identify potential warning signs to protect you from avoidable danger (i.e. inability to control anger).

ঙ্গ৩

*Hindrances left
unattended to
will continue to
negatively
influence you.*

Karen Maloy

ঙ্গ৩

9

Focus on your emotional and mental health

Take responsibility for your own peace of mind.

Our first responsibility in life is to ourselves. Although it sounds romantic, it places undue hardship on others emotionally when they have to be responsible for your mind as well. Get rid of any emotional baggage from past hurts and relationships so you do not punish the one that you have grown to love.

For your relationships to be right, they must start with right thinking.

Identify any misconceptions and areas of unrealistic expectations. If you are waiting for that perfect mate, then you are in for a rude awakening. There is no such individual. There was only one perfect individual who lived and that was Jesus. Perfection is the ultimate example of an unrealistic expectation.

A relationship ruled by your emotions is a life out of control.

While emotions are there to help us, they make a very poor foundation, as they are fickle and are prone to change based upon our circumstances. Making life decisions from this perspective is the basis of instability and the foundation for double-mindedness.

ଛଠଓଃ

Evaluation of your past relationships helps one to avoid emotional pitfalls in your future.

Karen Maloy

ଛଠଓଃ

10

Reflect upon your previous relationships

Your past relationships are the key to your future.

Your past relationships must be explored to identify any patterns of behavior which could potentially hinder your relationships. If you are not willing to look at your past relationships, you are setting yourself up to make the same mistakes in the future.

The only way to find your mistakes is to look for them.

Just as the root of the plant is unseen, so is the root of the problem. One must dig deep to discover the source of the true issue. While this often requires a process of digging, prodding, and sometimes emotional pain, it is a necessary step for relationship maturity.

No one is perfect! Not even you.

Know that you are to present the best you in a relationship, but also accept that you are human and will not be perfect. Willingness to accept your own imperfections will position you to accept others' imperfections as well."

Section 3
Relationship Building

ᏕᎧᏟᎧ

Who you yoke yourself up to now, will influence who you become in the future.

Karen Maloy

ᏕᎧᏟᎧ

11

Carefully choose a date who shares your godly beliefs

Understand the principle of being evenly yoked.

Being evenly yoked is not just a command, it is a principle. Once understood, you can avoid potential barriers which would serve as the source of conflict.

Compatibility is not limited to spiritual beliefs.

Great relationships do not happen by accident. While it is not impossible to do, any areas of incompatibility will place additional strain on an already laborious relationship.

Any differences not addressed prior to your commitment, may be the source of your demise.

Problems must be addressed sooner rather than later. Just like running water over a long period of time has the power to erode, the same is true for little problems which are left unattended. They will eventually ruin your relationship.

Section 4
Relationship Building

ഇഐ

Do not discount the power of attraction. It will serve as part of the foundation of your relationship.
Karen Maloy

ഇഐ

12

Focus on the qualities which you were attracted to

Identify those qualities/factors which attracted you to your potential mate.

People are to be celebrated for their uniqueness. Write down those characteristics that you were attracted to and keep it handy. This list will be useful during the challenging moments in your relationship.

Act quickly when detrimental behavior patterns appear.

Never assume that things will work themselves out on their own. If you do not address them when they occur, you will have to suffer with what you allowed to happen later.

Evaluate your potential mate based upon your relationship plan.

A relationship is a balance between two individuals meeting each other's needs. Take the time to reflect upon your list of *likes and dislikes* on a regular basis. This is the only way to assure that your needs are being addressed in the relationship as well.

ക്കരു

A relationship without any boundaries is like a ship tossed about in a midst of a storm.

Karen Maloy

ക്കരു

13

Establish reasonable and meaningful boundaries

Make the word of God the standard for your conduct.

It is not a matter of who is right or who is wrong. All behaviors, all decisions, and thoughts should be grounded in the word of God. This is what brings glory to God.

Your boundaries provide a safety net for your life.

Your boundaries are your invisible lines of protection. They provide a guideline for others to know where their responsibility begins or ends.

Create a list of what you will not tolerate in your relationship.

Your boundaries must be expressed to be adhered to. Make a list of your boundaries, and be willing to share them within your relationships. People can only be held accountable for what has been revealed to them.

അ൭ഄ

The time to plan for your future is now, in the future will be too late.

Karen Maloy

അ൭ഄ

14

Establish a specific time for you to reflect upon your relationship

Always make time for those things which are the most important to you.

Time is a valuable commodity which is a great equalizer. What separates us is our ability to manage it. We must be willing to invest time into those things which are the most important to us. If it is important to you, it is worth scheduling the time to reflect.

Identify unfavorable qualities, but focus on the favorable ones.

Identifying what you don't like will present potential opportunities for compromise, while focusing on the favorable ones will allow the good qualities to outweigh the bad.

Invest time in discovering their goals, dreams, and potential.

The greatest compliment you can give to another is to let them know that you are interested in who they are. Expect the same from them.

ഇരു

*Do not assume
that others
know what
you mean
because you
know what
you are
saying.*

Karen Maloy

ഇരു

15

Do not underestimate the importance of communication

Communication is God's plan for revealing his purpose.

God is the great communicator! He goes through great lengths to make sure we understands what He is saying, and he uses many methods. Using God's example of communication, you can potentially avoid many misunderstandings.

Good communication is the foundation for understanding.

People will never understand your point of view if you are not willing to express it. A single mode of communication is good, but the use of several methods will be great.

Do not assume that people know what you need if you haven't asked for it.

Assuming that someone knows what you need before you have expressed it places undue hardship on them to try to read your mind. While they may eventually get there in years to come, it is not without much time, effort, and endurance.

ഇ൭ൽ

*The purpose
of wise
counsel is to
protect your
life not to
control it.*

Karen Maloy

ഇ൭ൽ

16

Consider the reports of those who are qualified spiritual advisors

Do not underestimate the value of wise and qualified counsel.

Great is the man that can learn from the mistakes of others. Wise counsel can stop you from making some of the same mistakes if you would only heed.

Not everyone who holds a title is qualified counsel.

Not everyone who holds a title is wise counsel, for to be qualified one must have endured and overcome. Seek counsel from those who have evidence of these in the areas you are seeking, and be mindful of counsel from those who have not.

Eliminate unqualified people from your mentor pool.

Just a wise counsel can positively influence your development, unwise counsel can negatively influence it. Sometimes it is just best to sever those ties.

ഇൽ

If your identity is tied to your relationship, you are nothing less than confused.

Karen Maloy

ഇൽ

17

Maintain Your Life Balance

Your identity is your gift from God.

1 + 1 = 2 until you are married, after that, you can expect to always be working on the process of becoming 1. It is important however, that you never relinquish your identity to your relationship.

You were created for a divine purpose which will be use to add to your relationships.

The person God created you to be will be necessary to fulfill your life purpose. Your contribution combined with other believers will be necessary to fulfill God's divine purpose.

If a person cannot accept you for who you are, they do not deserve you.

No one likes to feel like a work in progress all of the time. If they cannot accept you for who you are, you are destined to a life to trying to live up to their expectations.

ଛଠଓ

Rome was not built in a day, and neither will your relationship be.

Karen Maloy

ଛଠଓ

18

Take your time!

Good things are worth waiting for.

Much like a seed uprooted before its time, if you are not willing to wait for the truth to reveal itself, you may end up with an unwanted harvest later.

The things which are the most important take the most time and the most effort.

To endure the joy of having a good relationship in the future, time must be invested in the foundation during the present. If you are not willing to sow it, you will not reap your due rewards later. In addition, be careful what you are sowing for you will reap those rewards.

Time invested now will avoid time-plus-money invested later.

Haste does make waste. Proper preparation can eliminate costly mistakes physically, emotionally, mentally, and financially.

Section 4
Before You Say "I Do"

ଚୀଔଃ

Do not be deceived. The apple which has fallen from the tree is either like it or influenced by it.

Karen Maloy

ଚୀଔଃ

19

Meet the family and friends

Family and friends offer a window to the interior.

Remember - the apple does not fall far from the tree! If your potential mate is not like their family, they are in the least influenced by it. Any stone left unturned will reveal its secrets later.

You learn a great deal about a person when you know who they spend their time with.

If you dislike many of their friends for the same reason, these may be the things that you will grow to hate in them.

Be mindful of those individuals who do not have any friends.

People are used by God to perfect us, and friends often challenge us. If we lack friends, we have not begun the process of working out our imperfections.

ಬಿಡ

*Do not assume
you are going
to the same
destination
because you
are traveling in
the same
direction.*

Karen Maloy

ಬಿಡ

55

20

Define and discuss your expectations for each other with each other

Identify what your future goals are for the relationship.

By taking this first step, you are conveying to your mate what your level of commitment is to the relationship.

Together create a written agreement which clarifies your individual expectations.

Although expectations may change over a period of time, this document serves a basis for agreement and accountability. Make it a point to revisit and update this document regularly - together.

Make a habit to discover opportunities to give into instead of taking from your relationship.

Although it is better to give than to receive, if both of you are not operating out of that principle someone is missing out. Make a conscious effort to balance out your relationship. Be sure that you are meeting the needs of your mate, as well as getting your needs met.

CONCLUSION

We have all heard that the definition of insanity is doing the same thing over and over again expecting different results. Given the state of marriages in our society, we can see that Christians as well as non-Christians are heading for divorce at an alarming rate. We must do something different!

As human beings act out of their belief systems, it is important to realize that if you want to change your actions, you must first change your belief system. Within this book, I have outlined 20 keys which I believe will be instrumental in helping you to be successful in your dating relationships.

I encourage you to continue to read these pages, study them prayerfully, and learn from them. These principles are based upon God's infallible word. If you make a decision to live your life based upon God's biblical principles, I can assure you that you are guaranteed success. So go forth in confidence knowing that you are now fully equipped to succeed in your relationship.

Happy Dating!

God Bless – Minister Karen

Appendix

Foundation Scriptures for Healthy Relationships

1. **Recognize the Importance that God places on your relationships.**

   Psalm 68:3

   But may the righteous be glad and rejoice before God; may they be happy and joyful.

   Ecclesiastes 5:19

   Moreover, when God gives any man wealth and possessions, and enables him to enjoy them, to accept his lot and be happy in his work—this is a gift of God.

   Hebrews 10:25

   Not forsaking the assembling of ourselves together, as the manner of some is; but exhorting one another: and so much the more, as ye see the day approaching.

2. **Understand that your relationships have a divine purpose.**

   Genesis 2:18
   The LORD God said, "It is not good for the man to be alone. I will make a helper suitable for him."

Colossians 3:12-14

Put on then, as God's chosen ones, holy and beloved, compassionate hearts, kindness, humility, meekness, and patience, bearing with one another and, if one has a complaint against another, forgiving each other; as the Lord has forgiven you, so you also must forgive. And above all these put on love, which binds everything together in perfect harmony

Proverbs 27:6
Wounds from a friend can be trusted, but an enemy multiplies kisses.

3. Discern that Satan is the enemy of your life.

1 Peter 5:8-9
[8] *Be alert and of sober mind. Your enemy the devil prowls around like a roaring lion looking for someone to devour.* [9] *Resist him, standing firm in the faith, because you know that the family of believers throughout the world is undergoing the same kind of sufferings.*

1 Timothy 6:6-10
But godliness with contentment is great gain. [7] *For we brought nothing into the world, and we can take nothing out of it.* [8] *But if we have food and clothing, we will be content with that.* [9] *Those who want to get rich fall into temptation and a trap and into many foolish and harmful desires that plunge people into ruin and destruction.* [10] *For the love of money is a root of all kinds of evil. Some people, eager for money, have wandered from the faith and pierced themselves with many griefs.*

Proverbs 12:26

One who is righteous is a guide to his neighbor, but the way of the wicked leads them astray.

4. Know how to activate your spiritual authority during times of demonic attack.

Genesis 2:18

A friend loves at all times, and a brother is born for adversity.

Colossians 3:12-14

Put on then, as God's chosen ones, holy and beloved, compassionate hearts, kindness, humility, meekness, and patience, bearing with one another and, if one has a complaint against another, forgiving each other; as the Lord has forgiven you, so you also must forgive. And above all these put on love, which binds everything together in perfect harmony

2 Corinthians 2:9-11

Another reason I wrote you was to see if you would stand the test and be obedient in everything. [10] Anyone you forgive, I also forgive. And what I have forgiven—if there was anything to forgive—I have forgiven in the sight of Christ for your sake, [11] in order that Satan might not outwit us. For we are not unaware of his schemes.

5. Pray for discernment daily.

Romans 16:17

I urge you, brothers, to watch out for those who cause divisions and put obstacles in your way that are contrary to the teaching you have learned. Keep away from them.

Matthew 7:15
Watch out for false prophets. They come to you in sheep's clothing, but inwardly they are ferocious wolves.

Revelations 12:11
They triumphed over him by the blood of the Lamb
and by the word of their testimony; they did not
love their lives so much as to shrink from death.

6. Make an Honest Assessment of Yourself

Hebrews 12:

See to it that no one falls short of the grace of God
and that no bitter root grows up to cause trouble
and defile many.

Luke 16:10

Whoever can be trusted with very little can also be
trusted with much, and whoever is dishonest with
very little will also be dishonest with much."

Matthew 7:24-27

Therefore everyone who hears these words of mine
and puts them into practice is like a wise man who
built his house on the rock. 25 The rain came down,
the streams rose, and the winds blew and beat
against that house; yet it did not fall, because it
had its foundation on the rock. 26 But everyone
who hears these words of mine and does not put
them into practice is like a foolish man who built
his house on sand. 27 The rain came down, the
streams rose, and the winds blew and beat against
that house, and it fell with a great crash."

7. Carefully plan what you want from your relationship

Psalms 119:59

I have considered my ways and have turned my
steps to your statutes.

Proverbs 24:27

Put your outdoor work in order and get your fields ready; after that, build your house.

Proverbs 24:27

Prepare your work outside; get everything ready for yourself in the field, and after that build your house. [27] *The rain came down, the streams rose, and the winds blew and beat against that house, and it fell with a great crash."*

8. Establish a list of what you will and will not tolerate.

Proverbs 14:12

There is a way that appears to be right, but in the end it leads to death.

Proverbs 14:26-27

Whoever fears the LORD has a secure fortress, and for their children it will be a refuge.

[27] *The fear of the LORD is a fountain of life, turning a person from the snares of death.*

9. Focus on your emotional and mental health.

Matthew 22:36-40

Jesus replied: "'Love the Lord your God with all your heart and with all your soul and with all your mind.' [38] *This is the first and greatest commandment.* [39] *And the second is like it: 'Love your neighbor as yourself.'* [40] *All the Law and the Prophets hang on these two commandments."*

Psalms 38:5

My wounds fester and are loathsome because of my sinful folly.

Proverbs 15:21

Folly is joy to him who is destitute of discernment, but a man of understanding walks uprightly.

Galatians 5:16-24

[16] *So I say, walk by the Spirit, and you will not gratify the desires of the flesh.* [17] *For the flesh desires what is contrary to the Spirit, and the Spirit what is contrary to the flesh. They are in conflict with each other, so that you are not to do whatever[a] you want.* [18] *But if you are led by the Spirit, you are not under the law.*

[19] *The acts of the flesh are obvious: sexual immorality, impurity and debauchery;* [20] *idolatry and witchcraft; hatred, discord, jealousy, fits of rage, selfish ambition, dissensions, factions* [21] *and envy; drunkenness, orgies, and the like. I warn you, as I did before, that those who live like this will not inherit the kingdom of God.*

[22] *But the fruit of the Spirit is love, joy, peace, forbearance, kindness, goodness, faithfulness,* [23] *gentleness and self-control. Against such things there is no law.* [24] *Those who belong to Christ Jesus have crucified the flesh with its passions and desires.*

10. Reflect upon your previous relationships

1 Corinthians 13:11

When I was a child, I talked like a child, I thought like a child, I reasoned like a child. When I became a man, I put the ways of childhood behind me.

2 John 1:8

Watch out that you do not lose what we[a] have worked for, but that you may be rewarded fully.

Ecclesiastes 7:20

*Indeed, there is no one on earth who is righteous,
no one who does what is right and never sins.*

11. Carefully choose a date who shares your godly beliefs

2 Corinthians 6:14

*Do not be yoked together with unbelievers. For
what do righteousness and wickedness have in
common? Or what fellowship can light have with
darkness?*

Amos 3:3

*Do two walk together unless they have agreed to
do so?*

Song of Solomon 2:15

*Catch for us the foxes, the little foxes that ruin the
vineyards, our vineyards that are in bloom.*

Matthew 5:22-25

*[22] But I tell you that anyone who is angry with a brother or
sister will be subject to judgment. Again, anyone who says
to a brother or sister, 'Raca, is answerable to the court.
And anyone who says, 'You fool!' will be in danger of the
fire of hell.*

*[23] "Therefore, if you are offering your gift at the altar and
there remember that your brother or sister has something
against you, [24] leave your gift there in front of the altar.
First go and be reconciled to them; then come and offer
your gift.*

*[25] "Settle matters quickly with your adversary who is
taking you to court. Do it while you are still together on
the way, or your adversary may hand you over to the
judge, and the judge may hand you over to the officer, and
you may be thrown into prison.*

12. Focus on the qualities which you were attracted to.

1 Samuel 16:7

But the LORD said to Samuel, "Do not consider his appearance or his height, for I have rejected him. The LORD does not look at the things people look at. People look at the outward appearance, but the LORD looks at the heart."

1 Peter 3:4
Rather, it should be that of your inner self, the unfading beauty of a gentle and quiet spirit, which is of great worth in God's sight.

13. Establish meaningful and reasonable boundaries.

2 Timothy 3:17

All Scripture is God-breathed and is useful for teaching, rebuking, correcting and training in righteousness, so that the servant of God may be thoroughly equipped for every good work.

Proverbs 4:23 & Matthew 7:6

Above all else, guard your heart, for everything you do flows from it.

Do not give dogs what is sacred; do not throw your pearls to pigs. If you do, they may trample them under their feet, and turn and tear you to pieces.

Hebrews 12:11
No discipline seems pleasant at the time, but painful. Later on, however, it produces a harvest of righteousness and peace for those who have been trained by it.

14. Establish a specific time for you to reflect upon your relationship.

Ephesians 5:15-16

Be very careful, then, how you live —not as unwise but as wise, [16] making the most of every opportunity, because the days are evil.

Romans 12:18

If it is possible, as far as it depends on you, live at peace with everyone.

Luke 6:31
Do to others as you would have them do to you.

Galatians 6:7

Do not be deceived: God cannot be mocked. A man reaps what he sows.

15. Do not underestimate the importance of communication.

Proverbs 18:13, 19

To answer before listening— that is folly and shame. A brother wronged is more unyielding than a fortified city; disputes are like the barred gates of a citadel.

1 Corinthians 2:11

For who knows a person's thoughts except their own spirit within them? In the same way no one knows the thoughts of God except the Spirit of God.Isaiah 26:3

You will keep in perfect peace those whose minds are steadfast, because they trust in you.

16. Consider the reports of those who are qualified spiritual advisors

Proverbs 19:20-21

Listen to advice and accept discipline, and at the end you will be counted among the wise. Many are the plans in a person's heart, but it is the LORD's purpose that prevails.

Romans 2:20-24

an instructor of the foolish, a teacher of little children, because you have in the law the embodiment of knowledge and truth— [21] you, then, who teach others, do you not teach yourself? You who preach against stealing, do you steal? [22] You who say that people should not commit adultery, do you commit adultery? You who abhor idols, do you rob temples? [23] You who boast in the law, do you dishonor God by breaking the law? [24] As it is written: "God's name is blasphemed among the Gentiles because of you."[

Proverbs 13:20

Walk with the wise and become wise, for a companion of fools suffers harm.

17. Maintain Your Life Balance

1 Corinthians 12:27

Now you are the body of Christ, and each one of you is a part of it.

Romans 12:3-8

[3] For by the grace given me I say to every one of you: Do not think of yourself more highly than you ought, but rather think of yourself with sober judgment, in accordance with the faith God has

*distributed to each of you. ⁴ For just as each of us
has one body with many members, and these
members do not all have the same function, ⁵ so in
Christ we, though many, form one body, and each
member belongs to all the others. ⁶ We have
different gifts, according to the grace given to
each of us. If your gift is prophesying, then
prophesy in accordance with your faith; ⁷ if it is
serving, then serve; if it is teaching, then teach; ⁸ if
it is to encourage, then give encouragement; if it is
giving, then give generously; if it is to lead do it
diligently; if it is to show mercy, do it cheerfully.*

Galatians 5:1

*It is for freedom that Christ has set us free. Stand
firm, then, and do not let yourselves be burdened
again by a yoke of slavery.*

18. Take your time. *Genesis 21:1-12*

*Now the LORD was gracious to Sarah as he had said,
and the LORD did for Sarah what he had promised. ²
Sarah became pregnant and bore a son to Abraham
in his old age, at the very time God had promised
him. ³ Abraham gave the name Isaac to the son Sarah
bore him. ⁴ When his son Isaac was eight days old,
Abraham circumcised him, as God commanded him. ⁵
Abraham was a hundred years old when his son Isaac
was born to him.*

*⁶ Sarah said, "God has brought me laughter, and
everyone who hears about this will laugh with me." ⁷
And she added, "Who would have said to Abraham
that Sarah would nurse children? Yet I have borne
him a son in his old age."*

*⁸ The child grew and was weaned, and on the day
Isaac was weaned Abraham held a great feast. ⁹ But
Sarah saw that the son whom Hagar the Egyptian had*

borne to Abraham was mocking, [10] and she said to Abraham, "Get rid of that slave woman and her son, for that woman's son will never share in the inheritance with my son Isaac." [11] The matter distressed Abraham greatly because it concerned his son. [12] But God said to him, "Do not be so distressed about the boy and your slave woman. Listen to whatever Sarah tells you, because it is through Isaac that your offspring will be reckoned. [13] I will make the son of the slave into a nation also, because he is your offspring."

Proverbs 21:5

The plans of the diligent lead to profit as surely as haste leads to poverty.

19. Meet the family and friends

Proverbs 22:6
Start children off on the way they should go, and even when they are old they will not turn from it.
Proverbs 18:24
One who has unreliable friends soon comes to ruin, but there is a friend who sticks closer than a brother.
Proverbs 27:17
As iron sharpens iron, so one person sharpens another.

20. Define and discuss your expectations for each other with each other.

Proverbs 24:27

Put your outdoor work in order and get your fields ready; after that, build your house.

Habakkuk 2:2

Write down the revelation and make it plain on tablets so that a herald may run with it.

Acts 20:35

In everything I did, I showed you that by this kind of hard work we must help the weak, remembering the words the Lord Jesus himself said: 'It is more blessed to give than to receive.

MUTUAL BLESSINGS BOOKS
HUNTSVILLE, AL
MBSUCCESS@KARENMALOY.ORG
WWW.KARENMALOY.ORG

* 9 7 8 0 9 8 5 6 6 0 8 1 9 *